OF
EMBODIES

OF
EMBODIES

philip sorenson

**RESCUE
+PRESS**

Rescue Press, Milwaukee 53212
Printed in the United States of America

www.rescue-press.org

Book design by Sevy Perez
First Edition
ISBN: 978-0-9844889-9-5

For Olivia

CONTENTS

LETTER   5

ELAGABALIUM I   33

FLOWERING BODY   49

ELAGABALIUM II   59

NOTES ON SOURCES   74

LETTER

others can rush out of the lakeside the resort town with news and an enormous load of recycling piled in their trunks the shadow of a fence behind them morning and stockinged legs wound birdlike the dandelion is as complete and as obvious as arrival and with flashlight in hand an extension of everything that has ever arrived there is another person living inside of you what could be more complete what could be added to a pig with bark in its stomach this dandelion is harmonious far into the shrieking cavity because there is nothing else "to glorify . . . glory is the manifestation of being as it advances in its magnificence as being, free of what conceals it, secure in the truth of its exposed presence."

PORNOGRAPHY IS SYNESTHETIC

and stuck to a sharp heel
and flattened and near flattened

the worry
it's singing and singing

all the cars in a long line the
insect crushed like a crane

all the cars

pistils and the sticky fluids coarsening

to starfish-like flakes and pins

the smell of fish frying

the trees and the eventide the memory the double medicine
an oracle found   a sidewalk oracle   and skin covers the city a
terrible flapping

gaily flapping its wings

if I could gather breathing into a pin a stiletto heel to crush forever the insect imagine the means: it must be an infinite point like an image in its weightlessness a coyote eating a rat a water filled light fixture and a crushing ever and forever their skeletons

the soft made rigid

an infinitely small point to shatter the ridgeofitsspine the wing and blue eyes phosphorescent see them horse-like pawing the glassy cords of bacteria stretched from the mandible through the digestive tract and excreted: a thread a fly

WHAT IS THE RELATIONSHIP BETWEEN GALACTIC EVOLUTION, TIME, AND KITSCH?

clearness lurches
and stops an ensemble

of infinitely diverse
machines: urine and evil

sniffing

time and ossification
into skin and milk and medusa

she shuffling into her cave
gliding between keys

teeth

stabbing the snow the birds
leave their wings

and carve us asleep
sawing and sawing

your skin will fall off
on stage on stage

your skin will fall off
to forest to vacate to go

[program] the scientist was betrayed by his wife who'd stolen his work
and sold it to the men who needed his formula for evil they tried to kill
him but his lab exploded and

think of it

all these thin horses

quivering horses

TEXT

we weave their parts and reap
the parents tethered down

in every consonant
they lay unmoving

we saw them up and wither each season each
serial remarkable and sad

we will take them and
examine their penises

we will saw each body into parts and birds will come
to eat the parts like pictures posted on the Internet

how will we be re-represented
what will stab us

what bodies fabricate

in terminal swell
a reflection on a polished spoon

I am just one skin a lecture
an articulation: a shame a mouth

TEXT

a kind of rest the sleep
of crabs or

a smooth half exposed
breast white and almost hen like

like white feathers like a paleness
cupped arousing the silent readers their brittle

screens of desiccated membranes the dried snake skins but still and divine:
an endless intercourse

an endless interiority the screen entombing each passenger with secretion
like a bear's head stuffed into a beehive

always entering a room the moment of entering reveals the meaning
of interiority of intercourse the yellow and dried skin as

consonants as pieces of fruit as penises that can be handled as
photographs that can be e-mailed as trees that grow at the edges of
fields and shade the vowels the white breast cupped and full of wind the
branches each hand moving the words the little photographic plates full
of fruit and meat and cats at an aquarium reading the shapes of the fish
and tongues learning to penetrate a word with the body to lean in and
whisper but meaning is a fleeing

therefore they toss on hair and lips to part they toss a sheet over
the man falling off his chair for brown shoes brown slacks

done what else done
meal eaten digested and digested

I mean digesting a meal

brown shoes brown slacks what else
what's done brown slacks my meal I mean

my dinner eaten when you're done it's digested
fabric wool sheer a body is just precedent

a man walks into a restaurant done
what else is there but mouths but fabric

a geography of wells and a geography of planes
drape the sheet cut a hole for the mouth

done the dining the dinner I mean
now it's inside the body what else done

the body I mean is severable by how much
a plane infected the making growing

like ice in a moustache an object
delivered as its own precedent

SUBJECTS OF DISCOVERY

no honeycombs dripping
guh guh guh

nothing for the toilet
no tongue

the hydra wave
in long dark lines

propping open
our mouths

the lips a finger

pulling sticks from the throat:
here the *y*, here the *f*, here the letter *h*

a certain kind of
inside

can be terrible we say up our catching
like species carry specimen

15

static guard speed stick long black hairs all of the soft skin there is nesting on floors in dark piles pajamas and a worm in a flood and white thighs and a worm in a door a curtain cutting in half her dress tucked in her nylons swaying through the slushy lobby shiny black globes and beetles' larvae it is January and a dryness a wetness reclines in the bed legs elevated white roping like string on a dressed turkey migrating toward a liminality a disappearance a degrading growth and then we stand a long night without sleep

AFTER-MEMORY

piles of jars
littered mayonnaise

jelly mustard
jars some muddy

or half full
some clean

and rows of airline
seats tangled

giant
animal jaws

everything half arranged
around us we've abandoned

we've been sleeping
it's drizzling

the tarp is ripped
and everything is wet

only later we hear
snoring

someone's

snoring drilling
there is depthlessness
everywhere

the crowds
that seem to head

someplace lined up
for something

our feet are wet
the endless shivering

the piles are
growing

new limbs mustaches
toenails anuses vaginas

spreading outward
toppled thing a blanket

an eating leaking growing
it is impossible to stop

soon the whole camp
will be gone

we will move under
the ground
and grow
blind

forgetfulness of history
an old angel curling

up a potato bug
and we will have

no memory there
it will never have been

no membranes no
sunny glistening

eyeless and tongueless
grub hunting leviathan

one forgotten
collective shade

swimming to chew
to mime itself

DOWN THE HATCH

A menace on the heads
of these little shivering nudes

little horses with little black eyes.
Pears half etherized.

Like a hand dangling
from a hospital bed, everything

seems perfect for eating.
On these long orchard walks

where fruit snaps under foot
and the stork with its pierced heart

feeds its young on maternal gore,
we rest under a tree as the world's

rim grows into heavy limbs
and climbs into our mouths.

bombardment after bombardment until the faucets lose their meaning
their trajectory their ends like the discovery of a bee asleep on a fallen
maple leaf after awhile you stop collecting they arrive in a comb

full of black hair

in the flies over the lilies the air in a tissue of yellow

I did not know I had such a beautiful mother size and age could not be supposed sitting at the table they bring the chowder and the bread and the wind animates the chimes and the cabinets and it seems to stretch and stretch with the satisfaction of an easy extraction one of many local representatives like the mold we need removed from our chimney no sound of trumpets will issue from the graves neither ghost nor dolphin will wander the shore or return to the first cave: memoria demnata

at the table sunlight the worms that
hide sleepless telekinetic

Lucifer with long stork-like necks
pruning many

warm grapey days imperial
the plaid the pregnant women

parading drying cooing in the sun relief a beetle
whines inside the Dixie cup

a pincer grabs a piece of meat
witness and inventor of the pumping lymph

the carrying of larvae across a leathery green
across the stiff the holly the white pellets

for bursting into forms into cramps moving down on us devouring the
smooth face

a memory of the tree springing from the saw
or a shadow that climbs the yard we dig up
to transplant we are digging up fingers
from our bodies the letter S rooting around in clay

a bicycle
a scarf

swelling
swelling

in the bushes
winds the clock

winding

and

winding

hair combed
straight a black waterfall

a hundred thousand holes
from the pale backs

climb an old woman
runs her nail across the card

the moon trucks away
all drowsy

24

the clicking overhead
the circling

naked now
vomiting a terrible

weight of meat
and hair

surrounds you
blue ink smeared

and difficult
to read standing

walking toward the road
it's all you could find

the traffic is very heavy
semi trucks delivery drivers commuters

drinking their coffees applying their makeup staring patiently ahead you wait
in the bushes crying to yourself how could you be here like this you are a fuck-
ing piece of shit aren't their blue suits twins they so perfectly not like you full
of shit the time in your bedroom listening to *Purple Rain* on CD your father
burst in slapped you as hard as he could right across the face that was a Sunday

you hid in your closet fell asleep in a pile of clothes the smell of the cut
grass all stuck together

in the
dumpster

behind
the K-Mart

a pair
of stretch pants

you did and that night a yellow star hung just under the moon's horn
everything still like a fly in sugar the geese standing

afternoon pink
push out the calf

elephantine gloom
of belongings piled

a fantasy horse
the boy rode

of pulsing hands
his sister called dear frog

a contemptible marsh
a false marsh

not the pale reeds
spread on soapy

bricks   hand reciting
the wheelchair's quiet

the shoeless feet
the rising and falling

rooms that stalk
out of us

noiselessly the car disappears up the ramp

nothing whatever but
is and cannot

ever not be   mute and quick the
pink canals, escalators

tottering invisible and then with violence
disgorged a fountain of machetes

the time and driving tongues
between the broad leaves

a pig and a dog

topple the trash

like paragraphs like bees climbing
over each other to unload

their baskets into the worm

THE WASPMEN IN THE PINES WILL TURN TO WATCH THE GASSING

Unbutton my shirt, crack my chest
(Theremin squeals)
and the antlered thing will rise
from my torso's cavity.

Wearing a crown of pelicans
and tallying the sand and stones,
it will fall in the street like snow
and crawl into the oven alone.

SUMMER

damnation of memory like royal portraiture or the beaked time travelers
recovered from Montana there's a shovel somewhere under the lilies we
used for plugging burrows but we'll need to wait until winter lingers
about unbroadcast under the illusion of a daily solar victory against
night which like the cold never was an autumn cavalry just restraint

your animal headed grandmother arrived
even she was standing in the garden digging

and the worm you found inside your underwear
drawer and the other witches we invented too

wind caught by the stresses of oratory

the branches sing with their nets and pits

we've been asleep for days

on our chairs

the moon is as thin as an arm

that's just been cut from a cast

stubbornly accrete weave

as if eaten

we found snails crawling on the screen a persistent ache covered in pulp
expectation is asleep in the abyss so we work with minor authorities: the
taxing responsibilities of pay stub and sex the occasional shell cracked
open or the door to the crawl space with flashlight and hammer but
nothing comes out of the holes under the walnut tree one might find frogs
or a waxy nude an imitation inside our own bodies buried

ELAGABALIUM

I

blood comes from pipes

bees sting cows
where corpulence built a honeycomb

a grim and gigantic woman

blamed for slaughter   was destroyed

and with each replacement a renewed disintegration
as if the sun could lose its grotesque face

it was just a pile of stones
or a tree's trunk and birds' eggs

I've put my fingers into
strangers' mouths

and stuck vocabulary
onto non-vocabulary

now she's legs and fingers
so why not try

these shoulders that keep the city
aright

in the sheep pen
changed terrified null

his mother's side

like a desert light
in an old polaroid

HIS BODY

the bridle
in your hand

no organs
no black art

crawls across
its sad infancy

cut me into certainty
into a thousand machines

oh varius she says

youthfulness pooling like skin
over bone and clouds in sky

her fingers find everything

she sighs and then sometimes interrupts

a delirious whistle

> lonely in his
> closet full of white leather shoes

seagull seagull seagull

INTERPOLATION

trunks and shoes and tires and broken monitors and turquoise leaking
from broken skin in flowing as in more geography than arrow the
disappearance we assume which is fiction or ekphrasis or error is your
body and the terrible heartache you barely remember which of course
is to say tautological what does it allow us except to know that progress
is just an aura an excrement from things and their passage we mistake
for gesture and so illusion and history like a weird ghost at your dinner
party after the guests have piled their coats on your bed and you find a
long blond hair growing from your forearm how could it have grown
so long without your noticing and yet here it is almost five inches and
nearly transparent and you pluck it and drop it into the toilet and flush
and now it's alone and the ghost appears at the table and points and
points and there is no choice you have no choice it is the knife inside the
knife the belly inside the belly

I first saw him

in his car waiting for
a canteen

my husband is a blonde
and violent man

his head is the sun
in its zenith there is a couch

and I pulled him into
the dim light

unpurpled and I
swallowed him whole

undefeated sun   stroll losing everything
but this black stone

have you lingered
in doors

                there's a pale
wrist a dart visible

oh

the sound of roosters like
everything half done

these sandals arrive   the gravel
so slightly at what temperature

mercury evaporates the most goldenest light
of morning

in coolest spring

gravel
purples everything   my skin these loose robes

and the enemy and the noise
to the leather   to be read

and directly published
our *common* preserver

he himself voluntarily
published this calumny:

the proofs of their plots I have not sent

it would be useless

as the men are already dead

he melted golden flies
into coins the size perhaps
of small Ferris wheels

44

depilated meticulously
the doctors have and cast

my chief enjoyment
is bareness

the widths of things
how they stretch

                  long pins drawn slowly from
a wig

words arouse me
and the smell of shit

dearest daughter
can you see why

I've always loved the mouth?
teeth on teeth

tongues, oh tongues
they appear on me

in gunmetal they appear
and banks of mud
they appear

I'll eat
I'll be dead soon

in my mouth
my tongue is moving

all set out varieties of the sidewalk and the whale
diverse wings

progress
from letter to letter

the shells on the tray especially

a worm swims from me
100 tails of flame and nerve

what is the sound
now baking in the desert

an interchange
an imaginary arrangement

a crawling across the
face making a new face

the fineness of rope

INTERPOLATION

to bring the sound the caravan as it moves toward Imperial time the sunlight as it must have sailed luciferian and the rattling of the trunks suggesting one of the boy's possible physical ends and what of the bodies stretched or leaning into or out of that desert light and everything moving toward incarnation as gesture in which the trunk of beheading was precedent a border before the hailing the speaking out as mimic *everywhere the text permeates* the body is silenced and we are left with the fascination of space the utterance into a trunk asleep warmly it was lined with red felt but far more it was the sound of the trees' insisting

FLOWERING

BODY

EXTERNAL OF TIME

a new membrane to fill that is filled and then in an instant a tearing
a new skin to be filled an infancy pregnant as rooms utterly full with
screens and people talking their lips never stop they're always moving
calling a boiling over and steam the trash the heaps of trash and everything
is full of leaking fluid of fluid leaking into my body I can hear the river
my bleeding nose

the reflection of a porcelain hand in a screen

a mouth opening and closing and the body it describes is the body

with the mouth with the words in the mouth

EXTERNAL OF TIME

the protuberance a boil growing to the point of bursting the skin

endless webbing and a portrait of the animal
building its nests covering the world

with the incrustation of syllables hanging like convicts

or clouds of wasps and they sting our faces and fight
and tug like foals to free their gametes all mouth

all mouth filling and spitting

what is the difference between the

tongues and their victims
languishing like enormous nudes on velvet couches

it makes you and you cannot help yourself and in the end there is no escape

standing over your body it points *here here here*

at the wall of growing an ominous the bracket the rodent's the otter's
eye

how am supposed to be how am we now in our leaking skins
the simile opening feeding on the on and on

scratching at the quarantine more mouths more subterranean feeding
more chains more "*a* miser . . . , *some* gold, more gold" what are we
when asked the trap already sprung the whale is rotting in the Everglades
the peacock opening its fan you have two hands with which to make a
category "racing along a witch's line"

FLOWERING

the trim of the world has brought

us to this

I plan
I forget

let us become coherent
without all the troubling

mute as the petals that shush

signlessly   flowering

aloft

OBJECT

we curtain
our humanity and close

our summer rooms

galls of paper

we have never been

do not believe

do not believe

empty out your mouth

into the starry cone

OBJECT

could dream us here and build telescopes with our hands I want to saw
out of the witch but she hangs on everything like the insistent eyes of
cows for example the rat that slinks by the building by the lilies and air
conditioner whips at us with its tail as it turns and columns of worms
spinning over and over buried in red drawers

LEVIATHAN

an observatory can watch
progression through disassociation

solitude is poisoned with me

silence and the trembling

let's unfix

our missing prisoner

a glowing worm in the chimney

commences its drone
then nothing

I cannot remember

ELAGABALIUM

II

URANIA

probing probing

far from the hacking and crushing

the blackberry bush where elderly soldiers milk
their frightened dogs

on the frozen river's edge

what a terrible bruise

           so ready to hang
between the world as it is and
whatever

lingers behind the sails

did you see it move
just now

a tail swung over the dunes

bag of milk

a baby asleep in a pelican's mouth

grasping her penis she dips a toe an ankle
her whole leg into the lake

fog descending

             a gibbon
feeding on the fingers

this thing wears military boots and a laurel crown
delightful

excavations reveal   1. golden bowl
                        2. ritual staff
                        3. human hand bones

crocodile headed child
give me your hand

fragile beetle's wing
we'll climb the hill together

SPECTACLE

the painted red face issues like a deadbolt
as if clenched in badgering pincers

[video]

a little fly an algae bloom
what screen   am   we   supposed to look at me

is stubborn facts of being   a   sad   dart   pierces

it is full of people

they are sleeping

INTERPOLATION

"The absence of time is not a purely negative mode, it is a time without negation, without decision, when *here* is also *nowhere*, when each thing withdraws into its image and the 'I' that we are recognizes itself as it sinks into neutrality of a faceless 'he.' The time of the absence of time is without a present. . . . The irremediable nature of what is without a present, of what is not even there as having been, says: that has never occurred, never a single first time, and yet it is resuming, again, again, infinitely. It is without end, without beginning. It is without a future." And so there is a body that is and yet it has ceased to be a body and we flee from ourselves in wounds and letters that hang around our genitals and mouths like so much sarcastic goading the kind that comes from our loved ones in our terrible dreams the end is not here which is a kind of everything that remembers when you were a child and were operated on when they took pieces of your body away but the nurses and nurses and nurses and nurses none real but ghosts of nurses and nurses arcing outward

laden ships sink
into the harbor

I am oppressed by the scale of it
and each fabrication

dedicated to a different primary color
among stacks of hay

once at sea

in the air
as ten brought ten thousand

six hundred heads   swimming down the canal
like something

no longer

his roundness has always reminded me of potatoes all full of mud

I have always loved only you
my rope   oh to be buried alive

ROPE

helicopter seeds
regale and regale

golden rod

oh throat

the moon on the gymnasium floor

this way is the whole cost:
ejaculation and orbit

the seeds flashing across
a frightened yellow face

a mollusk crawls under
the wood to live so the moon

a *meteorite* on the shoulders
of a hunched old man

Jupiter   it comes always
over the horizon

like a fleet of burning arrows
and stamps out the beds

drawing back the lid
spine

then the towers had
indiscriminately the gold

names are invisible pots

articulated
into grand sewers

remind those who have
only arrived

of the quiet

the armor is clattering

stacked like
glowing fungi

under darkened palms

MIDSUMMER

black stone

mother bent against daybreak's ram

and lingering under rafts of pigeons

doors invite arrows

where white horses march

there is no rider

the long   the winter sky

of indeterminate ends and fingers

of all your fingers stuffed inside of me like pigs

saying *truffle* and *blame me* and *I'm ashamed*

NOTES ON SOURCES

Elagabalus (born Varius Avitus Bassianus), the sexually ambiguous ancestral head of a Syrian sun cult, ruled from 218–222. Earnest Cary's translation of Cassius Dio's *Roman History* and Anthony Birley's translation of Suetonius's *Lives of the Later Caesars* provided material for some of these poems. The facts of Elagabalus's reign are unclear. Roman historians largely falsified materials as part of a propaganda campaign. Time and mendacity create a kind of material silence, like spaces before and after a question: a convex or diabolical quiet.

The poems on pages 7 and 66 include quotations from Maurice Blanchot. They are drawn from *The Station Hill Blanchot Reader: Fiction and Literary Essays* translated by Lydia Davis, Paul Auster, and Robert Lamberton. On page 15, a fragment appears from Barbara Johnson's translation of Jacques Derrida's *Dissemination.* The poem on page 53 includes quotations from Gilles Deleuze's "Literature and Life"translated by Daniel W. Smith and Michael A. Greco, and a distortion of a line from Henri Michaux's "Dragon" appears on page 47.

ACKNOWLEDGEMENTS

Thanks to Caryl Pagel and Daniel Khalastchi for their help in the shaping of this book.

Thanks, too, to those journals in which some of these poems previously appeared: *Action, Yes*; *Moria*; *elimae*; *Strange Machine*; *Wunderkammer Poetry*; and *Asymptote*.

RESCUE
+PRESS